Music and Musicians

Eva Bailey

Batsford Academic and Educational Ltd   London

Typeset by Tek-Art Ltd, London SE20
and printed in Great Britain by
R J Acford
Chichester, Sussex
for the publishers
Batsford Academic and Educational Ltd,
an imprint of B.T. Batsford Ltd,
4 Fitzhardinge Street
London W1H 0AH

ISBN 0 7134 1310 7

ACKNOWLEDGMENT

The Author and Publishers would like to thank the following for their kind permission to reproduce copyright illustrations: Mr R. F. Brien, fig 53; BBC Hulton Picture Library, figs 1, 8, 22, 29, 32, 35; BBC Photographs, figs 44, 45, 49, 50, 54, 55; The British Library, fig 4; British Tourist Authority, figs 25, 56, 57, 60; Burke Publishing Company Ltd, fig 7 (from *Songs Under Sail*); Sue Chapman, figs 13, 14; Decca Record Company Ltd, fig 58; Dewynters Ltd, fig 52; Dolmetsch, fig 46; Zoë Dominic, fig 59; Mary Evans Picture Library, figs 23, 24, 36, 40; Zena Flax, fig 12; Fodens Motor Works, fig 31; The Dean and Chapter of Gloucester, fig 38; Mandel Archive, figs 30, 39; The Mansell Collection Ltd, figs 2, 3, 6, 9, 11, 16, 17, 21, 26, 27, 28, 33, 41, 47, 48; National Portrait Gallery, London, figs 19, 37, 42, 43; Popperfoto, fig 51; St Paul's Choir School, fig 5 (photographed by Eileen Tweedy); Cecil Sharp House, fig 15; Victoria and Albert Museum, figs 20, 34. Thanks are also due to Patricia Mandel for the picture research on this book.

Contents

The
Illustrations

1
Early Music

Have you heard of St Cecilia? Today, choirs and other musical organizations often bear her name. She holds a very important position, for she is the Patron Saint of Music.

It was not always so and, although English legends existed about St Cecilia, for hundreds of years her name was not connected with music. St Cecilia was martyred in Sicily as long ago as AD 176, but it was not until the sixteenth century that the suggestion was made that Cecilia was the inventor of the organ. Paintings depict her playing various instruments including the harp and the organ. From then on, Cecilia was associated with music. It is from paintings, music manuscripts and other documents that we learn of the practices, the type of instruments and the ideas which people held about music in early times.

Musicians began to celebrate St Cecilia's Day, 22 November, in various ways, and they still do. Quite a number of music societies and groups of musicians use the name of their patron saint. You may have heard of the Saint Cecilia Singers and other organizations whose title includes the name "Cecilia".

The English celebration of St Cecilia's Day originally took place in London. Around 1700, the practice spread and celebrations also occurred in a number of provincial cities. These included the cathedral cities of Wells, Salisbury and Winchester, where concerts of classical music were performed.

But the main task of the musicians in the cathedrals was to perform sacred music as part of the religious services. For hundreds of years, the monasteries and the cathedrals were the main centres of music in England.

Sacred Music

The cathedral choirs sang the religious services in Plainsong. Plainsong is a single-line melody intoned in the rhythm of speech and sung in unison. As its name implies, there are no ornaments or florid passages. The origin goes back to early Christian times. It developed gradually, but notable advances were made in Plainsong on two occasions. The first occasion was in the fourth century, when Archbishop Ambrose of Milan standardised the Plainsong in use by fixing four scales which were to be used. Two centuries later, when Gregory was Pope, Plainsong was again reviewed. At this time, in addition to other changes, four more scales were added. These two kinds of Plainsong chants are known as Ambrosian and Gregorian.

Plainsong was introduced into England in the form of Gregorian chants while Gregory was still the Pope. These chants are still used today.

Settings of the Mass which was sung in all

▲
2   This chant for a psalm is from a psalter dated 1459. It is possible to see the relationship between the Plainsong shown here and the later development of the music score.

churches were eventually harmonized so that, instead of all the voices singing the same melody, each voice sang a different part.

When, between 1536 and 1539, Henry VIII suppressed the monasteries, a great disaster befell English music. In order to halt the religious musical activities of the monks, thousands of volumes of music were destroyed. Other volumes were sold abroad so that the parchment could be used for bookbinding.

◀1   In one of the legends about St Cecilia, she is reputed to have attracted an angel to earth by her music-making.

Another great disaster occurred during the Civil War. About 1642, Puritan soldiers ransacked some of the cathedrals, damaging the organs and destroying the music.

In these two catastrophes, most of the early English sacred music and the record of the practices of the monasteries and cathedrals were lost.

When Henry VIII ordered the closing of the monasteries, only the cathedrals were left as the main centres of music in England. Their importance in the musical world was enormous. To gain recognition and fame as a musician, it was necessary to obtain the post of a cathedral organist.

Colleges and academies for the training of musicians did not exist until the nineteenth century. Before that, in order that a boy with musical talent might receive tuition, it

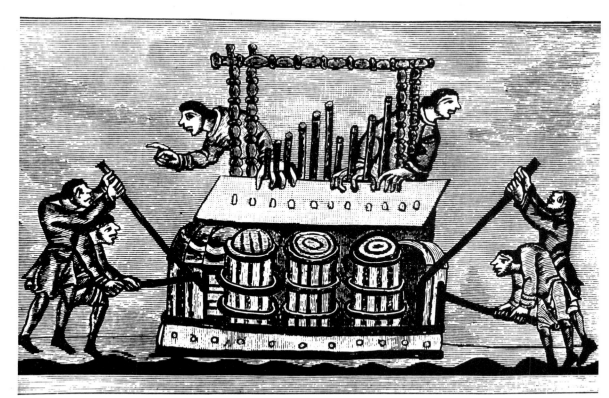

▲
3   Before it was possible to use electricity, air
had to be pumped by hand into the bellows of an
organ, in order that notes would sound. Four
"blowers" are working hard to supply this organ
with air. The instrument was in use from about
1130 to 1174.

was essential for him to become a cathedral
chorister. After several years, if he was
fortunate, he would receive organ lessons
from the organist. Then, if he reached a high
standard of performance, he would be
allowed to deputize for the organist from
time to time.

It is for this reason that most famous
English composers between the fifteenth and
the eighteenth centuries had a connection
with church music, usually being a cathedral
or church organist.

The progress of cathedral and church
music has not been steady. The use of organs
and choirs has alternated between periods of
favour and periods of unpopularity. In the
seventeenth century string and wind
instruments like viols and sackbuts were
used to play for sacred services.

During the Restoration Period, in about
1660, when the monarchy was restored to
the throne after England ceased to be a
Commonwealth, much organ-building took
place. There was then such a shortage of
boys' voices that instruments had to be used
in their place. Sometimes, organs and choirs
were abandoned because of financial
problems and other difficulties, but often it
was because those in authority decided that
they did not want them.

The Chapel Royal

One other important establishment was the
Chapel Royal, which was in existence at
least as early as 1135. This was not, as the
name might suggest, a building, but a group
of clergy and musicians which was required
to perform before the King. The Chapel

8

Royal still exists today, although the duties are somewhat different. Nowadays, the members of the Chapel Royal lead the Sunday services which are usually held at St James's Palace, but sometimes at Buckingham Palace or Marlborough House in London.

Relations between the cathedrals and the Chapel Royal were not always friendly. For almost two hundred years during the sixteenth and seventeenth centuries, the equivalent of our modern talent spotters would travel to various cathedrals, listen to the choirs, and take the best singers for service with the Chapel Royal. The rule was that only the best choristers were good enough to sing before the King. Because of this, the cathedrals were robbed of their best voices.

Once a boy became a member of the Chapel Royal, he was not treated royally, but had a very hard time. Because of their time-consuming musical duties, the boys received little general education. This situation continued into the nineteenth century. Sir John Goss (1800-80), who became a famous composer and was organist of St Paul's Cathedral, was a member of the Chapel Royal as a boy. He was well aware that general education was neglected, and said:

4 This picture was painted in the early fifteenth century to illustrate a book of Bible stories. It shows instruments which were used in churches, including buzine, recorder, lutina, shawm, harp, vielle, kettledrums, trumpet, rebec, lute and psaltery.
▼

Although the main centre of early music was the cathedral and church, and all the music sung at the services was sacred, some recreation was found in singing and playing secular music. The earliest known English composition of this type is "Summer is icumen in", and this song is still sung today.

Sumer is icumen in,
Llude sing cuccu;
Growth sed and bloweth med,
And spring'th the wude nu,
Sing, cuccu!

The words are in the dialect of Wessex, but in more modern English would be:

6 The old manuscript of "Sumer is icumen in". This song, written centuries ago, is still popular today.

▼

▲
5 Maria Hackett (1783-1874) visited every cathedral in the country in her endeavour to improve the life and conditions of the boy choristers.

We had a writing master from half-past twelve to two on Wednesdays and Saturdays, if my memory does not deceive me, and no other instruction in reading, writing and arithmetic and a little English Grammar than we could get out of the time.

The same kind of situation had also been prevalent in the cathedrals during the eighteenth and nineteenth centuries. Miss Maria Hackett (1783-1874) became aware of the young choristers' hardships. She was a wealthy lady, and used her time and her money in order to improve the life of choir boys throughout the land.

Summer is a-coming in,
Loudly sing cuckoo,
Groweth seed and bloweth mead,
And springs the wood now,
Sing cuckoo!

There is some doubt about the actual date of composition, but this complicated six-part song was known to exist in the thirteenth century, when John of Fornsete, a monk at Reading Abbey, wrote it down. The original manuscript is now at the British Museum in London.

Madrigals, unaccompanied songs for several voices, were introduced by the Chapel Royal in the reign of Elizabeth I. This was when the Chapel Royal reached the height of its success. Although the madrigal was not a piece of religious music, it was similar to some of the motets and anthems sung in the churches. The words of the madrigal are often romantic, or describe the glories of nature and the countryside. The music is usually written in five or six parts with one voice to each part, and sung unaccompanied.

In the street or the countryside, the ordinary man would also hum a tune, or play a simple instrument like a pipe, but a lot of this early music was never recorded. The melodies were passed down from father to son, and inevitably became altered or lost over the years.

2
Music of the Common Man

Sea Shanties

Music, particularly singing, has always helped the ordinary man in his arduous tasks. The men in sailing ships worked in time to the rhythm of the sea shanty. The name of this type of song is probably a corruption of the French word *"chanter"*, meaning "to sing", but the true English definition of a shanty is a sailors' working song. The verses of this were sung by the shantyman, who was employed especially for this task, and was excused all heavy duties. While the men laboured together to turn the capstan or pull on the rigging, they worked in time to the shantyman's singing, using their breath only to join in the chorus. Since the words of the chorus were the same throughout one song, the men were able to concentrate on their work. Sea shanties like "Blow the Man Down" had various versions of the tune, and it was quite common for the words of the shanty verses to be altered. One version is as follows:

Shantyman: Oh, blow the man down
bullies, blow the man down!
Chorus: Way-hay, blow the man
down.
Shantyman: Oh, blow the man down
from Liverpool Town,
Chorus: Oh, give us some time to
blow the man down.

Another well-known shanty is "What shall we do with a Drunken Sailor?"

Shantyman: What shall we do with a
drunken sailor?
What shall we do with a
drunken sailor?
What shall we do with a
drunken sailor?
Early in the morning.

7   The shantyman sang the verses of the song to lead the sailors as they worked. This one could also play his instrument.
▼

Chorus: *Hooray and up she rises,*
                Hooray and up she rises,
                Hooray and up she rises,
                Early in the morning.

Different sets of the verses were often vulgar or uncomplimentary to the ship and those in command. Since the verses were sung only by the shantyman, the sailors hoped that this one voice would not reach the ears of the captain or any passengers aboard. With the development of steam ships in the mid-nineteenth century, the need for the shantyman and his song began to decline.

Military Music

Just as music helped sailors to work together rhythmically, so, too, for centuries, it has helped soldiers to march along at a steady pace. Often they marched to the rhythm of the drum. Various instruments like the fife (a shrill shrieking pipe which was the forerunner of the flute) were added until, in the late seventeenth century, the full military band became popular. As well as drums of various kinds and other percussion instruments, the military band included woodwind and brass instruments. This is the basis of the military band which exists today. The combination of instruments can be varied, depending upon what is available. It is of prime importance that a correct balance of tone is achieved — too many big drums and loud instruments with low sounds would easily swamp the sound of instruments with lighter, softer tones.

Marches were composed, which were used on special occasions, and some of these are in a collection of pieces for the virginal called *My Lady Nevell's Booke*, which dates from the end of the sixteenth century. The music was written originally for a military band. The band would play the particular march which belonged to each contingent (footmen, horsemen, etc.) as the soldiers marched along. Yet another march would be played before all the troops went into battle.

▲

8   The Band of the Welsh Guards plays while marching through London in August 1917, during the First World War.

The proximity of different regiments would be recognized by the sound of a particular march, for example, the well-known tune of "The British Grenadiers".

If soldiers had no instruments to help them to march along, they had their marching songs, and these have always been very popular. In 1900, when Queen Victoria was on the throne, British troops were besieged in Mafeking during the South African War. Mafeking was relieved after 218 days, and not only the soldiers, but the general public as well, jubilantly expressed their pride and patriotism in the marching song, "Soldiers of the Queen", by Leslie Stuart:

13

It's the soldiers of the Queen, my lads,
Who've been, my lads, who've seen, my
*   lads,*
In the fight for England's glory, lads,
Of its world wide glory let us sing.
And when we say we've always won,
And when they ask us how it's done,
We'll proudly point to every one
Of England's soldiers of the Queen.

In the First World War (1914-18) several songs were great favourites of the troops. These included "Pack up your troubles in your Old Kit Bag" and "It's a long way to Tipperary".

Through the ages it has been found that marching music, whether played or sung, helped to ensure smart and orderly marching. It also kept the soldiers cheerful and, as a result, they did not so easily become tired and exhausted.

While ceremonial marching (for example, at the Trooping of the Colour) still takes place today, the mechanization of warfare means that it is not now normal to march armies on foot in order that they may take part in battle. Perhaps some other form of soldiers' music will evolve because of this.

Street Traders

The soldiers and sailors were not the only ones to have their own particular kind of music. The musical cries of the street traders in London are famous. These were known to exist as early as the fourteenth century and the song "Who'll Buy my Sweet Lavender?" could still be heard half way through the twentieth century. Each of these calls, whose rhythm fitted the syllables of the words, had its own tune. The muffin man, the tinker, the seller of eels and many others all had their own distinctive cries.

Musically, some are very beautiful, especially those of the flower sellers. Unlike the music of the cathedral and church, these cries had a strictly commercial purpose — to enable the singer to sell his or her wares.

9   "Round and sound, five pence a pound!" The cherry seller's cry was once familiar in the streets of London.

One cry has not yet died out. It is the call of the newspaper seller. This cry, sometimes with unintelligible words, serves the same purpose as the more musical cries of old.

Perhaps the most familiar modern equivalent of the old street cries is not sung. It is the mechanized tune of the ice cream man, each ice cream trader having his own particular signature tune.

Signature tunes on the radio and the jingles of the television advertisements could also be counted as an extension of the old street cries. Their purpose is the same — to attract the attention of the public and to sell merchandise.

Street Musicians

Musicians have often entertained people in the streets. Small groups of musicians called buskers, who became popular early in the twentieth century, can still, on occasion, be

10   The One-Man Band plays many different
instruments at the same time.

heard performing on street corners. Alternatively, a soloist will perform on his violin or other instrument. Solo buskers are regularly seen and heard today in London Underground stations. The One-Man Band was another type of busker, which was popular during the early part of the twentieth century, but which is rarely seen now. The people were not impressed by the quality of music produced in this way, but by the contortions often undertaken by the performer. The man would often blow a pipe, play a fiddle, bang a drum or cymbal by means of a cord connecting the instrument to his foot, ring bells by shaking his head, and play as many other instruments as possible, all at the same time.

Street musicians have rarely found favour with those in authority. During the reign of Queen Elizabeth I (1558-1603), they were regarded as undesirable characters. Those who sang and sold ballads (poems which were sung and which recounted historic and other important events), players of street organs and pianos, brass bands and other street musicians found themselves regarded as a disturbance and a nuisance.

Over the centuries various laws have been passed to curtail their activities. In Queen Elizabeth's reign, two Acts of Parliament were passed, declaring street musicians "rogues and vagabonds". Today, the Metropolitan Police Act, which was passed in 1864 and the Municipal Corporations Act of 1882 are still in force. These enable a charge to be brought against a street musician by a householder who complains that a nuisance is being caused.

Country Dance and Folk Song

Country people sang songs connected with their work. These often referred to the seasons or to the different highlights of the farming year, such as harvest or sheep-shearing time.

After work was done, countryfolk in the sixteenth century would gather together and dance, often to the music of a fiddle. In summer, these country dances were performed on the village green. Many were figure dances, where any number of couples moved through a sequence of geometric figures, sometimes in a circle or in a straight column. Two of the best-known dances are called "Strip the Willow" and "Sir Roger de Coverley".

The fiddle also accompanied the Morris Men. This team, normally consisting of six male dancers, performed in the country, often on May Day. Although Morris Dancing is recorded as early as 1594, it is still popular in many parts of the country. Different villages have their own dances and variations

11 The Ballad Singer would also sell his songs. He was an unpopular figure with those in authority.
▼

LONG-SONG SELLER.
"Two under fifty for a fardy!"
[From a Daguerreotype by BEARD.]

▲
12   May Day celebrations are still an annual event in many English villages. The children here dance to the music of the School Band.

13   The girls plait the ribbons round the Maypole as they dance.
▼

▲
14 These jovial Morris Men still perform in Oxfordshire.

of costume, although the dress usually includes hats adorned with flowers, gaily coloured ribbons being much in evidence.

Each dancer carries a white handkerchief in each hand, or one or two sticks. Strapped to his shins are strings or pads of bells. These items are all used to mark the rhythm of the dance.

One explanation of the name "Morris" is that it came from the term "Moorish". This is quite likely, since at one period one of the team of dancers used to blacken his face to make it look as if he was a Moor — a man with a dark skin who came from Morocco.

The Morris Dance is also thought to be a development of the Sword Dance. This is an elaborate figure dance, again for a team of men. Each man carries something to repre-

sent a sword — either a blunt sword, or a wooden replica or a flexible strip of steel with a handle at each end. Each dancer grasps the end of his own sword and also that of his neighbour. After much jumping over and passing under, the swords are finally locked together in a design which can be held aloft by holding the handle of just one sword.

The dances all have a rural robustness, and contrast greatly with the delicate movements of court dances of the sixteenth and seventeenth centuries.

By the early part of the twentieth century, many of the country dances and folk songs were beginning to die out. This was partly because they had not been written down and also because of rapid social change. At this time, people moved around the country more than previously and the population was growing. Cecil Sharp (1859-1924) was a professional musician. He became aware that Britain was in danger of losing part of its heritage — the national folk music. Sharp gave up his post as Head of the Hampstead Conservatory of Music and devoted his life to collecting as many of these old tunes as he could. He travelled to remote villages, and when he found someone who knew an old song, he persuaded the man or woman to sing it to him. Often an old person remembered something taught to him as a child by his grandfather. There were no tape recorders at this time, so Sharp listened carefully, and wrote down the notes on music manuscript paper and then copied down the words.

Cecil Sharp was also concerned that the English Country Dance should not be lost. Many years before, in about 1650, a book had been published called *Playford's English Dancing Master.* It is an important work and describes the steps and tunes of many dances of the time, both in the country and the royal court. Sharp studied this and eventually re-published it. The book is the basic guide to English dancing.

In 1898, the Folk Song Society was formed, followed in 1911 by the Folk Dance Society. They eventually amalgamated to become the English Folk Dance and Song Society. The work of the society is to foster an active interest in the traditional folk music of England, and festivals, courses and examinations are among its activities. As a tribute to the man who rescued so many of the songs and dances that were nearly lost, the name of the society's headquarters in London is "Cecil Sharp House".

15   Cecil Sharp collected folk songs in England and many other parts of the world. Here he is writing down a folk song in the Appalachian Mountains, Kentucky, U.S.A.
▼

3
Music of the Court

Minstrels

Under some circumstances commoners were able to provide music for courtiers and the nobility. In the Middle Ages, minstrels travelling from place to place visited large houses. A minstrel would accompany himself on a small harp and often sing his own verses. Like the ballad singers, minstrels carried news of the day. The ballad singer was also the ballad seller and he sold his wares on the streets, mostly in London. Both ballad singer and minstrel related stories and heroic or historic deeds of the past. Minstrels sometimes travelled together in a group, which could include a juggler. In Tudor times, beautifully carved minstrels' galleries were built into many mansions. They were placed high up along one wall and were obviously intended to accommodate a number of instrumentalists, whose music could be enjoyed by the gentry below.

Court Dances

Royalty and noblemen liked to employ their own musicians, the number of performers often depending on the wealth of the head of the household. Apart from performing to a listening audience, these players would take their place in the minstrels' gallery and accompany the dancing of their master and his guests. The dances were usually very

stately and dignified. Through the ages, different dances have reached the height of popularity. Until the seventeenth century, the Pavan and Galliard were favourite court dances. It then became the practice to adapt a country dance and make it suitable for gentlefolk to perform.

The Minuet made a great impact in the eighteenth century and, in addition to being a dance, it was included as a movement of some orchestral compositions. Another popular dance at this time was the Gavotte.

In the nineteenth century many new dances appeared. The Waltz, originating in Vienna, swept through England, as it did

16 Minstrels played in galleries similar to this in England and many parts of Europe.

▼

▲
17   The Minuet was a favourite dance during the eighteenth century.

through the whole of Europe. Dances of the gentry became much more active and lively, and others which came from the Continent included the Polka, the Quadrille, the Schottische and the Mazurka. Today, many ordinary people still enjoy these and other dances in various forms, using the term "Old Tyme Dancing".

Music-Making by the Court

Kings, princes, lords and their ladies were keen to make their own music. They would sing madrigals together. These songs were often complicated and difficult. It was considered a desirable accomplishment to be able to perform on various instruments. During the reign of Elizabeth I (1558-1603) stringed instruments like the viol, which was played with a bow, and the lute, which was plucked, were very popular.

Flutes of various kinds were also played.

End-blown flutes belonged to the family of instruments we now know as recorders. They existed as early as the Iron Age in the form of simple pipes made from bone, and eventually developed into the modern clarinet and oboe. In Tudor times, various types of end-blown flutes were played.

Side-blown flutes were also in use at this time. These were the forerunners of the orchestral flute which is known today, and which was perfected by Theobald Boehm in the nineteenth century.

The instrument which Queen Elizabeth I liked to play was the virginal, a rectangular keyboard instrument which was placed on a table. The mechanism of this instrument caused the strings to be plucked, in order to make the sound. The instrument was at one time thought to have been named after Elizabeth I, who was known as the Virgin Queen. This is not so, as the virginal was in existence before the time of Elizabeth. However, the instrument was considered very suitable to be played by young ladies, since the sound was sweet and quiet, and no doubt considered to be lady-like.

21

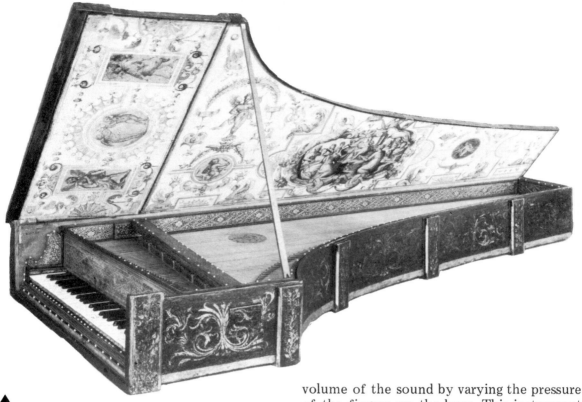

▲
18 This virginal belonged to Queen Elizabeth I.

Before the invention of the virginal, from the fourteenth century onwards the clavichord was played. This also had a keyboard, but the strings of this instrument were struck (not plucked), to make the musical notes sound.

As time went on, however, it was through the virginal that developments in keyboard instruments began to be made. After the virginal came the spinet which, with further improvements, became the harpsichord. In the case of the rectangular virginal, only one string played when a key was depressed; but two or more strings were sounded by each key of the curved harpsichord, so making the music louder. It was quite usual for a harpsichord to have two or even three keyboards. Various pedals or "stops" (knobs, which look similar to those on many organs) controlled the number of strings which were plucked. Even with all these additions, it was still not possible to control the quality or volume of the sound by varying the pressure of the fingers on the keys. This instrument has only limited ability for the sound to be sustained or held on. Because of this, music composed for the harpsichord usually contained a continuous pattern of short running notes.

After a performance lasting an hour or more, a harpsichord needs to be retuned. In the early models, the quills which plucked the strings also required frequent replacing. Some gentlefolk employed a tuner to tune and repair their instrument at very frequent intervals. Others took a pride in doing this themselves.

In recent years, a new interest in early instruments has arisen, and public concerts are given and broadcast with increasing regularity.

Harpsichords, lutes, recorders and other instruments are manufactured today at the business run by the Dolmetsch family in Haslemere, Surrey. There are also other manufacturers of early instruments, especially harpsichords, in England.

The music the gentry loved to play on

their different instruments included the tunes of various dances. Quite often these were named after courtiers and had titles like "Sir John Grave's Galliard" and "The Lord of Salisbury his Pavan".

Many English monarchs were very able musicians, either as performers or as composers, and sometimes as both. Henry V (1413-22) was a composer, while Henry VIII (1509-47) is notable both as a very able performer and as a composer. His daughter, Elizabeth I (1558-1603), inherited her father's love of music and played the lute as well as the virginal.

The well-to-do people took their music seriously. Samuel Pepys (1633-1703) wrote in his famous diary: "At noon played on my theorbo." A theorbo was the largest form of lute, which had a double peg box. When Samuel Pepys was a boy, his father taught him to play the bass viol. Samuel Pepys' love of music lasted all his life and he bought and

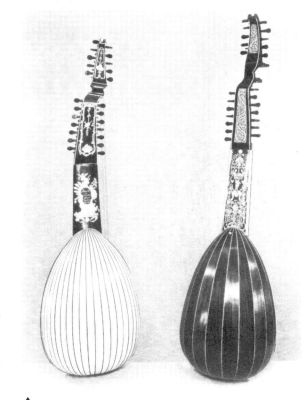

▲

20   Samuel Pepys often played the theorbo. The double peg box with two sets of pegs can clearly be seen.

19   Frederick, Prince of Wales, and his sisters are portrayed making music together. Philippe Mercier painted this picture in 1733.

▼

▲ **21** Thomas Tallis (1510?-1585). His music is still sung and played today.

learned to play many other instruments. These included the flageolet (an instrument similar to a recorder), the lute and the violin. Singing and dancing teachers were engaged for both Pepys and for Elizabeth, his wife. "Music is the thing I love most," he once said.

Early Composers

Many composers in the fifteenth, sixteenth and seventeenth centuries had connections with the Chapel Royal. In addition to performing and writing music for the church, these men also composed other music.

Thomas Tallis (1510?-1585) wrote some music for strings and for the keyboard, but is still remembered for the famous Tallis' Canon, now sung to the words "Glory to thee my God this night".

Tallis was organist of the Chapel Royal, jointly with his pupil William Byrd (1543-1623). Byrd was regarded as the most able composer of his time. He wrote music for the church, for keyboard instruments and for choirs.

Three notable composers were also gifted performers. John Bull (1562-1628) and Orlando Gibbons (1583-1625) were both brilliant keyboard performers. John Dowland (1562-1626) was a great lutenist. His compositions were mainly for voice with lute, or four part vocal works.

John Blow (1649-1708) wrote songs and harpsichord pieces. His music is still played today. It is thought that Henry Purcell was once a pupil of John Blow.

Purcell (1659-1695) ventured further from church composition than most. He composed music for the theatre, as well as instrumental and choral pieces.

All the composers mentioned above, with the exception of John Dowland, held an appointment as organist with the Chapel Royal. Dowland served Charles I as Court Lutenist.

The Chapel Royal, controlled by the reigning monarch, dominated and influenced English music during many reigns. During the sixteenth and seventeenth centuries England was the foremost European country in the composition and development of keyboard music and madrigals. The peak was reached in the time of Henry Purcell.

Royalty and Music

Music was important at any royal funeral. At the funeral of Henry VII in 1509, many musicians were engaged, including performers on the sackbut, shawm and trumpet. Thirty-eight years later, at the funeral of Henry VIII in 1547, the instruments included viols, a fyfe, a harp and bagpipes. When Queen Elizabeth I died in 1603, the musicians at her funeral included players of violins, flutes, hoboies, fifes, lutes, trumpets, sackbuts and drums. On each occasion the gentlemen and boys of the Chapel Royal took part.

Monarchs were proud to have their own private musicians and during the reign of Charles I (1625-1649) the post of Master of the King's (or Queen's) Musick was created. From that time until the reign of Edward VII

22 The boys of the Chapel Royal, in their scarlet dress, arrive at Westminster Abbey for the rehearsal of the Coronation of King George VI in 1937.

(1901-10) the holder of the position was in charge of the royal instrumentalists, who often formed a band or orchestra. The Master of the King's Musick was required to arrange concerts for royal events, often in conjunction with the Chapel Royal. Since then, there has not been an orchestra. It is now usual for the holder of this great honour to compose music for special royal and national occasions.

4
Opera, Oratorio and Orchestra

The Beggar's Opera

Every year from 1133 to 1855 a famous fair was held in Smithfield, London. It was St Bartholomew Fair. Business was conducted at this fair, held once a year, but it also provided amusement, a friendly meeting place and the opportunity to hear music. "Musick booths" were erected and one could go in to hear an orchestra or an ensemble of instruments or singers. At the end of the seventeenth century and the beginning of the eighteenth century, ballad-operas were performed at St Bartholomew Fair. In these, the spoken word alternated with song.

It was in 1728 that *The Beggar's Opera* was first produced in London, and later that year it was performed at St Bartholomew Fair. *The Beggar's Opera* contained popular music of the time, and included folk song and dance tunes. It also parodied the gentler airs of Purcell and George Frederick Handel. While *The Beggar's Opera* was an original work and was English, it also satirized the number of Italian operas that had flooded into England.

The Beggar's Opera came into being in 1728 and was a protest and a revolt. It was everything that Italian opera was not. In contrast to Italian opera, *The Beggar's Opera* was vulgar, its theme was low life and the common people and its characters were

▲
23 Many booths were erected at St Bartholomew Fair, including those in which music could be heard.

criminals. Not only did it ape Italian opera, but it struck out at political corruption which was prevalent in England. It was certainly not intended for gentlefolk's entertainment. But the shock which *The Beggar's Opera* imposed on England did nothing to lessen the performance of the Italian type of opera, nor did it open the way, at that time, for a truly English type of opera which was acceptable to all.

24 *The Beggar's Opera*. The theme of criminal, vulgar life is shown in this prison scene.

Italian Opera

Italian opera has little or no spoken word and is a story set to music. The story is sung, partly by soloists, partly by groups of singers or a chorus. Often the action of the story is carried along by recitative, in which the singer sings the words to definite notes, with a reasonable freedom of timing. Italian composers used a pastoral (or country) theme for their operas, or based them on Greek mythology. The operas were written to entertain the aristocracy. Many were performed in England in the early eighteenth century. It is from this form of opera that modern opera has developed.

Covent Garden

Many Opera Houses were built in Italy and Germany, but only one notable theatre was specially built in England for the performance of opera. That was in 1732, when Covent Garden Theatre was built in London.

25   The third building of the Covent Garden Theatre in London was opened in 1858, and is shown in this picture. It is the one which is still used today. The original theatre, built in 1732, was burned down, as was the one which replaced it.

▲
26 Five outstanding composers of the seventeenth and eighteenth centuries. William Croft (1678-1727) composed church and instrumental music. Although he is perhaps not now as well-known as the others in the picture, his church music is still used and his harpsichord music was re-published in 1921.

Whereas Opera Houses on the continent were mostly supported and financed by the state or the German princes, Covent Garden was not, and consequently the seats there were very expensive.

Henry Purcell

Henry Purcell (1659-95) was the most outstanding composer of his time. He was held in high esteem, not only in England, but throughout Europe. He wrote music for the violin and cello, instruments which were newly developed at that time. In his opera *Dido and Aeneas*, he surpassed even the continental composers of the day, and this opera is still frequently sung. After the death of Henry Purcell in 1695, when he was only thirty-six years of age, little progress was made in English music.

George Frederick Handel

George Frederick Handel (1685-1750) arrived in England from Germany when his opera *Rinaldo* was performed in London in 1711. Although a German, Handel wrote his operas in the Italian style. Handel returned to England in 1712 and made it his home. In 1726 he became a naturalized citizen. He wrote many more operas in the Italian style. Some of his operas were successful and others were not, but Queen Anne so enjoyed his work that she granted Handel a royal pension.

When, at the age of fifty-two, Handel suffered a severe illness, it appeared that his musical career was at an end. But this was far from true. Handel recovered, and instead of composing more operas began to compose oratorios. In this type of work, passages from the Bible are set to music. Oratorios are performed by solo singers and a choir, accompanied by an orchestra which often includes an organ or a harpsichord. It is not so expensive to present as opera, since it requires neither scenery nor costume. After composing *Saul*, and *Israel in Egypt*, Handel wrote *Messiah*. This was to become his most famous work. Handel felt inspired as he composed *Messiah*. He scarcely stopped even to eat during the three to four weeks in which he wrote it. He said:

I did think I did see all Heaven before me — and the great God himself.

The work was first performed in Dublin in 1742 and then in London in 1743. The King, George II, who was present, was so moved by the magnificent "Hallelujah Chorus" that he stood up as a mark of respect for the great music. Since the King had risen to his feet, the whole audience was

28

▲
27   George Frederick Handel at the height of his success.

The orchestras which played for the operas and oratorios would most likely be conducted by the musician who played the harpsichord. Handel frequently did this at performances of his own works.

The viol was gradually replaced by the violin, but during the transition it was not unusual for both instruments to be included in the same orchestra. The viol, which is held between the knees, has a sweeter tone than the violin, which is held under the chin. The violin has much more power and a brilliant tone.

Modifications also took place to other instruments of the orchestra. Towards the end of the eighteenth century, the basis of the modern orchestra had been laid. The string instruments are the foundation, with sections for brass, wind and percussion instruments.

New Music

Special music was composed for the orchestra, some of it for royal and national occasions.

Handel composed *Water Music* for a royal party in 1717. Fifty musicians were in one of the two royal barges, and they played the music as the guests sailed down the River Thames.

George II commissioned Handel to write *The Music for the Royal Fireworks* when a huge display was given to celebrate the signing of the Peace Treaty of Aix-la-Chapelle.

More and more concerts of instrumental and orchestral music began to be attended by those who could afford to go. Some people still loved the old type of English music and were anxious that it should not be forgotten. In 1710 an Academy of Ancient Music was formed. Its concerts often excluded Handel's works, as they were felt to be too modern.

Thomas Arne and William Boyce

Also in 1710 were born two men who were

also obliged to do so. This practice continues today. When the "Hallelujah Chorus" from *Messiah* is sung, the audience always stands. *Messiah* is a long work, and it takes over three hours to perform the complete score.

Handel composed many more oratorios, and although his other music is still heard today, *Messiah* is regarded as his masterpiece. He was, at the time, the only composer in England who wrote outstanding oratorios.

The Orchestra Emerges

Early in the seventeenth century more and more instruments began to be added to the groups that played together, and so eventually the orchestra emerged. Scores were written for whatever instruments were either in vogue or available. Orchestras often included a harpsichord. This was particularly necessary if singers were being accompanied by the orchestra, as the harpsichord played the chords for recitative to be sung.

to become noted English composers. Thomas Arne (1710-78) wrote several oratorios and operas, and a masque which included "Rule Britannia", with its patriotic words which are still sung:

Rule, Britannia,
Britannia rules the waves,
Britons never, never, never
Shall be slaves.

Arne also composed music for the theatre and his songs include settings of Shakespeare's verses.

William Boyce (1710-79) was the master of George III's orchestra. He composed music for both the church and the stage. In later life he became deaf. After that, he concentrated on making a collection of some of the finest English church music.

Concerts and Concert Orchestras

During the eighteenth century, musical concerts were given in various parts of London. Often these were not open to the general public, but those who went were specially selected or were members of the group sponsoring the concert.

Gradually, concert-going became more

28 This is an early version of the National Anthem, written by Dr Thomas Arne in 1745.

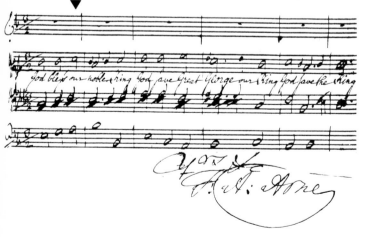

popular and orchestras were formed which still exist. In 1813, the Philharmonic Society was founded in London in order to foster good orchestral music. From its formation, symphonies, concertos and other large-scale instrumental works were regularly performed. Although formed mainly for the benefit of professional musicians, seats for the concerts were made available to others. The title "Royal" was granted to the Philharmonic Society in 1912, when it reached its centenary.

The interest in orchestral music spread to the provinces. The Liverpool Philharmonic Society was founded in 1840. It became the Royal Liverpool Philharmonic Society in 1957.

Although musical concerts were held in Manchester from the mid-eighteenth century, it was not until 1857 that Sir Charles Hallé formed the famous orchestra there that bears his name — the Hallé Orchestra. Associated with this is the Hallé Choir.

Changes were taking place. From the beginning of the eighteenth century the piano had gradually superseded the harpsichord as the most popular keyboard instrument.

The piano was a development of the earlier clavichord. The strings of both the piano and clavichord are struck, whereas those of the virginal, spinet and harpsichord are plucked. About 1709, Cristofori, an Italian, invented a *"gravicembalo col piano forte"* — a harpsichord with soft and loud. But the name was not strictly correct. Cristofori had used hammers to strike the strings and not, as in the harpsichord, quills to pluck them. The term *"pianoforte"* (soft and loud) eventually became the name of the instrument.

Cristofori's invention was shaped like an enlarged harpsichord, and was the forerunner of the grand piano which is now in use. Various adaptations and improvements were made over many years in different parts of the world. A square piano was made, but this is now a museum piece. Eventually, in 1829, Robert Wornum Jnr., in London,

perfected the upright piano.

After the era of conducting from the harpsichord or piano, the method of directing an orchestra changed. Conductors began to use a baton. An element of showmanship began to appear. The conductor, sometimes seated in a gilded chair, faced the audience. Wearing white kid gloves, he often used a heavy jewelled baton. Since he had his back to the orchestra, his beat was of little use to the musicians. Eventually this exhibitionism ceased and, during the second half of the nineteenth century, the conductor faced the orchestra. In addition to controlling the tempo of the music, he indicated how the different parts of the composition should be interpreted.

But the greatest change of all had happened — a great interest in concert-going had arisen among the general public.

▲
29   This early piano by Cristofori is shaped very much like the earlier harpsichord.

5
The Victorian Scene

Music in the Pleasure Gardens and Parks

Although most musical performances in the eighteenth century could only be attended by the privileged and well-to-do, in London varied entertainment at a more reasonable charge was provided by the pleasure gardens at Vauxhall (1660-1859), Ranelagh (1742-1803) and Marylebone (1650-1776). Different kinds of evenings were arranged including

30 The Vauxhall Gardens in the eighteenth century. The orchestra can be seen in the bandstand.

firework displays and dancing, but musical performances were very important. Orchestras played what are now termed "popular classics". These included waltz tunes, melodious arias from the operas, and other favourite compositions. The best musicians were engaged. Often a solo item was included which showed off the virtuosity of the individual performer.

While the music played, the audience walked round the gardens, enjoying not only their beauty and a lovely evening, but, of

▲
31 The Elworth Silver Prize Band. In 1902 this became the famous Foden's Motor Works Band.

32 Eastbourne bandstand and promenade in Queen Victoria's reign.
▼

▲
33   Salvation Army bands played regularly in late Victorian times and still do so today.

course, the music. The French word *"promenade"*, meaning "a walk", was adopted for this activity.

Both the Marylebone and Ranelagh Gardens ceased to exist by the beginning of the nineteenth century, but the Vauxhall Gardens continued until 1859, well into Queen Victoria's reign. The music there was enjoyed by people of all classes.

Listening to the Band

In the provinces, especially in Victorian times, parks were laid out with flower-lined paths along which to walk. The focal point was, however, the bandstand. On summer Sundays, after hearing music in church in the morning, Victorian families would walk round the park in the afternoon and listen to the band.

When George IV was Prince Regent he visited Brighton and had the Pavilion built in 1784. Gradually, other coastal holiday resorts and inland spas developed. By the middle of the nineteenth century they became very popular. Everything was provided to enable the visitor to enjoy his stay. Promenades along the coast and at the inland spas were

built, and a bandstand was usually in a prominent position. Concerts were very frequent in the holiday season in the summer months. Military bands from famous army regiments like the Coldstream Guards were engaged to give concerts. Brass bands and silver bands, mostly from northern England, gave concerts in bandstands on sea fronts and in parks. Many were prize-winners in competitions, and were associated with collieries or factories. The instruments of these military or brass bands made more sound than the concert orchestras which included stringed instruments. The bands had huge instruments, like the euphonium. Lively marches were always a great favourite, and since the men always wore either military uniform or the special band uniform, they were an impressive sight.

Sometimes the music in the bandstand was played by a small concert orchestra, consisting of strings, woodwind, brass and percussion, but this type of orchestra usually had another setting.

Pavilions and Winter Gardens

Many seaside resorts had ornamental piers built over the sea, where holidaymakers could walk out and benefit from the sea air. There was often a Pavilion or Winter Garden on the pier. This was usually a large structure

34

▲
34   This cover for the programme of Gilbert &
Sullivan's Opera, *Patience*, was printed in 1881.

bound to hear in late Victorian times was
that played by the Salvation Army. This
military-styled religious movement was
founded by William Booth in 1878. Although
serious in its religious fervour, the Salvation
Army used some unorthodox ways by which
to attract people to worship. One was to sing
words of a religious nature to a popular tune
of the day. Many of the sacred songs and
hymns used by the Salvation Army had
catchy tunes and rhythms, but were not of a
high musical quality.

The Army always had a band to lead its
outdoor services. As the movement became
established in various parts of the country,
there were more than one thousand Salvation
Army bands. These proved to be an excellent
training ground for many musicians.

Victorian Light Opera

More music was reaching more and more
people. Victorians made a point of going to

35   Marie Lloyd (1870-1922) was a very popular
Music Hall star.
▼

with numerous panes of glass. Tropical
plants, cacti and palms were displayed
around the rows of seats. Pavilions were also
a feature of inland spas. It was in these buildings that the concert orchestra performed.

Light popular music was usually played,
although as time went on some ambitious
orchestras, though small, included a symphony or a concerto in the programme from
time to time.

The Salvation Army

One kind of music which the public was

▲ 36   Victorian families enjoyed making music together at home.

listen to the band. Professional musicians seemed to play everywhere.

A new kind of opera began to appear which appealed to the Victorian public. It was more of a musical show than the aristocratic type of opera. The story was spoken, and linked by melodious songs and other musical items. It descended from the old ballad-opera, of which *The Beggar's Opera* was the forerunner. The new form of light opera avoided vulgarity and was acceptable to Victorian taste. Full of sentimentality, it was termed "English Opera". Among the most popular were *The Bohemian Girl* by M.W. Balfe, which was produced in London in 1844, and *Maritana* by W.V. Wallace, which was staged in the capital a year later.

But a great delight was still in store for Victorians. When Arthur Sullivan (1842-1900), composer of serious music, teamed with librettist W.S. Gilbert (1836-1911), the result was a stream of successful light operas. The works had liveliness, pathos, humour and charm. Although the setting might be in Venice or Japan, the operas were typically English, and gentle fun was poked at the English way of life and even at the government of the day. The success of Gilbert and Sullivan was enormous and, apart from a three-year gap when the two men had a quarrel over an insignificant matter, a steady stream of works poured out from 1867 until 1896. All the operas were popular, two of the most successful being *The Mikado* and *The Gondoliers*.

Following the success of *Trial by Jury* in 1875, Mr Richard D'Oyly Carte (1844-1901), an impresario and theatre manager, formed the D'Oyly Carte Opera Company to perform Gilbert and Sullivan operas. With the profit he made, D'Oyly Carte built the first theatre in London to have electric light — the Savoy Theatre. The Gilbert and Sullivan operas were produced at the new theatre, and the company of singers became known as the Savoyards.

The Music Halls

A sector of the Victorian public was also attracted to the Music Halls. These originated as musical events in the taverns of the sixteenth century, but developed in Victorian times into a show produced at a theatre. Various items were performed at each show. These often included comic songs, tunes played on a peculiar instrument such as a musical saw, impersonations and dances, all of which were presented in a glittery, showy fashion. Although some of the music was tuneful, most of it was poor in quality. The songs often gave a satirical glimpse of the times. Many regarded the Music Halls as low-class and not quite respectable.

Some people were much more attracted to the orchestral concerts. Many liked the light operas which were termed "musical comedies".

37 John Curwen (1816-80). The system he devised gave singers who were not able to understand a normal score the ability to sight-read music.

Music at Home

Radio and television had not been invented, and the Victorians had to provide their own home entertainment. Having heard the music, they wanted to make it themselves. People began to sing and, in particular, to play the piano. Every home which could afford one purchased a piano.

Family and friends would gather together and spend the evening music-making. What had been the mark of gentility among the upper classes now came within the reach of most ordinary people. The Victorians gathered in the parlour to perform to the assembled company. It was more informal than in Regency times, but the children of the family would be expected to play their "piece".

A suitor would thrill as his young lady sang a popular air. Four bashful youths would attempt to sing a well-known quartet — perhaps "Sweet and Low" by Sir Joseph Barnby (1838-1896).

In addition to the actual performance, much time was spent in practising. Since many of the tunes the public heard were overtures, symphonies and other forms of music scored for orchestra, simplified versions for piano only or piano and one other instrument were rapidly published. Special pieces were written, like "Alice, Where Art Thou?" by Joseph Ascher, and "Tarantella" by Sydney Smith, which would show off the player's virtuosity. Volumes containing an assortment of pieces written and arranged for the piano suddenly became available, one of the most popular series being the "Star Folios".

A new kind of ballad came into being — the Drawing Room Ballad. Although this had its roots in the old English ballad of earlier centuries, in Victorian times it was often a shallow, sentimental song, with a refrain or chorus repeated after each verse. Once a drawing room ballad had been sung — almost featured — at a concert by a well-known professional singer like Sims Reeves, vast numbers of amateur singers would purchase a copy in order to sing the song the next time there was occasion for singing in the parlour. The Victorian ballad was not usually composed as a work of art, but more as a business proposition for financial gain.

Although the works written at this time tended to be sugary, they certainly helped amateur musicians to improve their standards. Some became quite proficient, and the gap between amateur and professional narrowed.

Singing

Choirs and choral societies were formed during the nineteenth century. Some were for professional singers, but others were made up entirely of amateurs.

John Curwen (1816-80) discovered a teacher who used a moveable doh to help in sight-singing, and he perfected and promoted the method. In this, the name "doh" may be given to any note of the octave. The ascending notes of the scale from that doh are called ray, me, fah, soh, lah, te, doh. The final doh is an octave above the original doh. Since any note in the octave can be used as doh, it is possible to sing a tune written in any key. The system enabled thousands of people to sight-read difficult music, even though they had little knowledge of the printed score.

Church Music in Victorian Times

While there was much music-making in Victorian England, the quality of composition did not progress to any great degree.

During this same period, the performance of sacred music in cathedrals and churches became slovenly. Very little money was spent on purchasing music, sometimes services were chanted instead of sung, and there was little variation in the repertoire. Many choirs were depleted or even disbanded and all church musicians were badly paid.

However, during the late Victorian period a number of notable performers and composers of church music were very active. These included Sir Joseph Barnby (1838-96) and Sir John Stainer (1840-1901). Stainer's choral work *The Crucifixion* is still sung by church choirs today. The work of these composers, while sound, reflected the taste of the Victorian era.

Two composers whose work has a deeper-lasting quality are Sir John Goss (1800-80), who was organist at St Paul's Cathedral, and Samuel Sebastian Wesley (1810-76). Wesley was another musician who was a boy chorister at the Chapel Royal. As an adult, he became organist in turn of four cathedrals. He held high ideals and was very much aware of the low standards in church music. He was not afraid to work to achieve a higher quality of music in cathedrals and churches. However, his determination to fight official-dom and a tendency towards eccentricity caused him to be disliked by some. Even so, Samuel Sebastian Wesley did succeed in improving the performance of sacred music and raising the esteem in which it is held. His own compositions are of a high quality.

During Queen Victoria's reign, one step forward in the welfare of cathedral choristers was made. The Education Act of 1870 made sure that these boys received a good general education as well as musical tuition.

It is, however, true that in the Victorian era development in classical music was slow, and little progress was made.

▲
38   Samuel Sebastian Wesley (1810-76) was considered the finest organist of his time in this country.

38

6
The Flowering of English Music

Concerts at the Crystal Palace

During the second half of the nineteenth century, concerts were given every Saturday afternoon at the Crystal Palace. The building was an enormous structure, mainly composed of glass panelling. It was built in Hyde Park to house the Great Exhibition of modern industry and invention in 1851, then re-erected in Sydenham in 1854. Concerts were first given there in 1855.

39 The Crystal Palace, so called because it contained so much glass. Unfortunately, this magnificent structure was destroyed by fire in 1936.

The conductor of the Crystal Palace concerts was a German, August Manns (1825-1907). Many conductors at this time, anxious to gain popularity, presented entire programmes of light classical music. August Manns did not blindly follow this pattern. He also included in each programme a new or unfamiliar work. The public welcomed the opportunity to hear the new music. Concert-going at the Crystal Palace became a custom for music-lovers.

Music Colleges

About the middle of the nineteenth century

40 This is the setting of the Handel Festival, when it was held at Crystal Palace at Sydenham in 1859.

the education of professional musicians began to take a big step forward. In 1822, the Royal Academy of Music was founded in London. Courses were, and still are, provided in practical and theoretical musicianship. Successful students are awarded a diploma, the Licentiate of the Royal Academy of Music, entitling them to put the letters L.R.A.M. after their names. Students train either as a performer or as a teacher.

In 1873, a National Training College of Music was founded, also in London. Ten years later, this became the Royal College of Music. In the same way as the Royal Academy of Music, the Royal College of Music provides various courses for the training of musicians.

By 1900, more establishments for the education and training of musicians had been founded in the capital. These included the Royal College of Organists (1864), Trinity College of Music (1872) and the Guildhall School of Music and Drama (1880).

In the provinces, the Royal Manchester College of Music was founded in 1893, becoming the Royal Northern College of Music in more modern times.

At last there was a wider training ground for British musicians.

English Music

Gradually, new music began to be produced by English composers. Two men who were outstanding at the beginning of this improvement were Hubert Parry (1848-1918) and Charles Villiers Stanford (1852-1924). Although others later surpassed them, the work they produced was acclaimed as good-quality music. Parry's work was recognized as being typically English. His compositions were not based on folk melodies, but his works had a style which became recognized as English. One composition in which this is evident is his setting of Milton's poem, "Blest pair of Sirens".

Stanford, in addition to writing secular music, composed the setting of the Anglican church service known as "Stanford in B flat". This has become a standard work in the field of church music, and is still used today.

The period of stagnation in English music was over. The works of Parry and Stanford opened the way for others to develop and improve still further the music composed in England.

An element of nationalism began to creep into music all over Europe. Traces of traditional and folk music began to appear in new compositions. Composers were expressing their pride in their own country by including in their compositions references to its traditional music. This nationalism was also appearing in English music. Cecil Sharp and others were eagerly collecting original English folk tunes and writing them down for future generations. This provided a source of traditional music on which composers could draw and on which they might base their new music.

The new generation of English composers did not merely copy the old folk melodies. They based their modern compositions on typically English forms of music. Some of the works re-echoed the influence of Tudor times; some composers adapted the old medieval methods and structures. Despite reflections of old English music, the new generation of composers used original ways of expressing their music, and began to break away from restrictive rules.

Edward Elgar

Perhaps the most outstanding composer in this new era of music was Edward Elgar (1857-1934). Among his numerous orchestral compositions, his *Enigma Variations* are extremely popular. These pieces are musical pictures of people he knew. The writing is so cleverly carried out that, at the time, it was possible to identify those represented by the music. One was the frivolous "Dorabella", who in real life was Dora Penny.

Variation XI of the *Enigma Variations* bears the initials "G.R.S.". This was George Robertson Sinclair, the organist of Hereford Cathedral. In the piece, one can imagine the pedals of the organ being played, and at another point one hears the splash of Dan, Sinclair's bulldog, barking as it falls into the River Wye. And yet the whole is an orchestral composition.

The popular "Nimrod" variation depicts A.J. Jaegar, the author of the notes on Elgar's oratorios. In the music, this friend of Elgar's walks with dignified step across the room.

The other variations all follow the same pattern of representing in music the characteristics of Elgar's friends, and also his wife.

Elgar wrote *Cockaigne*, a concert overture which was sub-titled "In London Town". In this, his music represents the dignified bustle of the English capital.

Among many forms of musical composition, Elgar included oratorio. His setting of *The Dream of Gerontius* to words by Cardinal Newman is very different from the Handelian type of oratorio. Elgar's music has mystic qualities, which many people find very moving.

Gustav Holst

Another composer who played a major part in the advancement of English music was Gustav Holst (1874-1934). Holst was English, although, as his name indicates, his ancestors were Swedish.

Like Elgar and others, Holst made use of folk music in some of his work. In other compositions, he was very forward-looking. His orchestral suite *The Planets* was modern music for his time and did not revert to Tudor or medieval influences. This remarkable music was written before man success-

▲

42   Gustav Holst (1874-1934), a contemporary of Elgar's, studied music and composition at the Royal College of Music.

fully ventured into space. Holst's other compositions include opera, orchestral works and pieces for smaller combinations of instruments.

Holst also made a great contribution to music by his teaching. He was for many years Director of Music at St Paul's School, London. The quality of music while Holst was there reached an exceedingly high standard.

◀41   Sir Edward Elgar (1857-1934). Elgar's father was an organist and kept a music shop in Worcester. Even so, Elgar was largely a self-taught musician, but he became one of England's greatest composers.

Ralph Vaughan Williams

Ralph Vaughan Williams (1872-1958) is another composer who did much to contribute to the new, high-quality English music of the late nineteenth and early twentieth centuries. Pastoral and country topics often feature in his work. His song "Linden Lea" is a great favourite, as is his orchestral music entitled *The Wasps*.

Vaughan Williams wrote some typically English operas, including *Hugh the Drover*, *Sir John in Love* (based on the story of Falstaff), *Riders to the Sea* and *The Pilgrim's Progress*.

Sometimes Vaughan Williams turned to past centuries. In this earlier style, he composed a *Fantasia on a Theme of Thomas Tallis* and *Five Tudor Portraits*. He was a great supporter of the English Folk Song and Dance Movement, and was always keen to try new ways of expressing English music.

▲
43   Ralph Vaughan Williams (1872-1958),
pictured towards the end of his life.

Music and the Cinema

While English music was gradually climbing
to a new peak of achievement, other
mechanical and scientific wonders were
emerging. One, the cinema, developed from
William Friese-Green's jerky moving pictures
invented in 1885, passed through the era of
silent films and into the development of
modern sound techniques.

When silent films were screened for the
general public, it soon became obvious that a
background of music was needed. This was
to indicate and enhance the mood of the
action — joy, tragedy, excitement, horror or
thrill. The music was originally provided by
a pianist or a small instrumental group, and
was adapted to suit the film as it was
screened. Eventually it became the vogue to

44

have an organ installed in the cinema for this purpose.

These cinema organs were not of the same high standard as the great cathedral or church organs. Many economies were made. The cinema organ usually had numerous gadgets and could imitate a bird warbling, or even represent an orchestra. The quality of the sound produced was often poor.

It must be remembered that while the film could be mechanically reproduced for each performance, the accompanying music had to be played "live" for each showing of the film.

Things changed when improvements were made to the gramophone, which had been developing since Edison demonstrated his mechanical device in 1877. It became possible for music on gramophone records to be played as a background to silent films.

Another big step forward was made when synchronized sound films began to be produced in the early 1920s. The music could now be recorded with the film. It was possible to have more suitable music of a higher quality, some of it specially composed. Also, the sound was perfectly timed to fit in with the action of the film.

This was a new opening in the field of music. Film music was composed, some of it written by the new generation of specialists in twentieth-century English music. Vaughan Williams was one of these, and among his film music is that written for *Scott of the Antarctic*.

The First Promenade Concerts

The new works of English composers, many of whom studied at the Royal Academy of Music or the Royal College of Music, were often performed at the Queen's Hall. This concert hall was built in London in 1895. Henry J. Wood (1869-1944) was appointed to take charge of the Promenade Concerts which were to be held there. Henry Wood, who became Sir Henry Wood in 1911, held the post for the remainder of his life. He

44 The last night of the Proms, 12 July 1981. Despite all the fun and carnival atmosphere, the musical performance is of a very high standard. This concert was given by the BBC Symphony Orchestra conducted by James Loughran.

▼

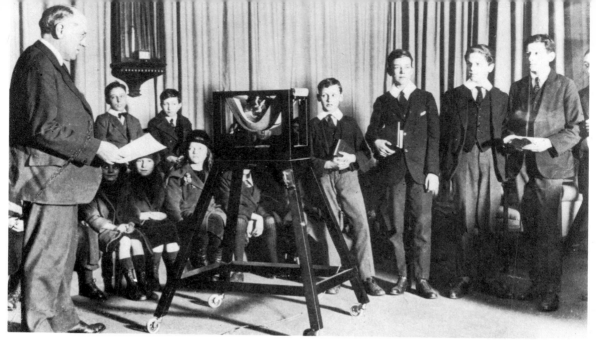

▲

45   Sir Henry Walford Davies (1869-1941) giving
the first broadcast music lesson to schools on 4
April 1924. The boys, who took part in the
broadcast, are choir boys from the Temple Church
in London.

planned and conducted the concerts for over
fifty years.

The work was a continuation of the concerts held in the Vauxhall, Marylebone and
Ranelagh Gardens, and those which took
place in the Crystal Palace. The programmes
did not consist only of popular classics;
many important works were also played.
Henry Wood included compositions which
were unknown to the concert-goers. He gave
living British composers the opportunity to
present the first performance of their works.

Various programmes, including some on a
special theme, were arranged and on 22
October 1901 the first "British Night at the
Proms" was held. The programme consisted
entirely of works by living British composers.
Music by Cowan, Stanford, Coleridge-Taylor,
Mackenzie, German and Parry was played.
But the most acclaimed work on this
occasion was the first performance of
Edward Elgar's "Pomp and Circumstance
March" No. 1 in D, which included the tune

of "Land of Hope and Glory". It has
remained a popular favourite at the Promenade Concerts ever since.

The progress in English composition at
this time, including the nationalism and the
folk tune influence, led to further experi-
menting in new forms of orchestration and
the use of harmonies.

The First Radio Broadcasts

Another important development which was
to affect music was the invention of radio.
Work to perfect the development of trans-
mitting sounds by radio waves had progressed
from the beginning of the twentieth century.
In 1922, the British Broadcasting Company
was formed and radio (or the "wireless" as it
was then known) became available to the
general public. Five years later, the company
became the British Broadcasting Corporation.
Music, including opera, was included in the
programmes transmitted.

One very important broadcaster was
Henry Walford Davies (1869-1941). This
able musician and composer was Professor of
Music at the University of Wales in Aberyst-
wyth. Walford Davies used the radio as a
means of giving nationwide music lessons.
His first broadcast music lesson to schools

was transmitted on 4 April 1924 and the series lasted until 22 June 1934. By means of his radio work, Walford Davies gave the experience and love of music to a whole generation of children. Although the work has undergone various progressions and alterations, music programmes for schools are still a major item on radio and television.

So successful was Walford Davies' work that in 1926 a radio programme for adult listeners began. It was entitled *Music and the Ordinary Listener*. A new nationwide interest in music had arisen.

Arnold Dolmetsch

Just as Cecil Sharp was eager to collect the old folk tunes, Arnold Dolmetsch (1858-1940) had a great interest in old instruments. It was in 1889 that Arnold Dolmetsch found an old manuscript in the British Museum. It was chamber music for viols. He wanted to play the music, but in order to do this he had to rescue and repair some of these old instruments. He was also interested in other old instruments, and built his first clavichord in 1894 and a harpsichord a year later.

Arnold Dolmetsch gave concerts on old instruments. He had a fine recorder, which was unfortunately lost when his son Carl left it in a bag on Waterloo Station. Arnold Dolmetsch decided that the only way to replace it was to make his own, and this he did. It was some time later that the lost

46   Craftsmen in the Dolmetsch Workshops at Haslemere in Surrey carefully make an early keyboard instrument.
▼

recorder turned up and was restored to him.

After a period abroad, in 1914 Dolmetsch settled in England and opened workshops for the manufacture of old musical instruments at Haslemere, in Surrey. Although still interested in other instruments, he worked to perfect the making of various types of recorder. By the end of the Second World War (1939-45) he had succeeded. In addition to those made of wood, recorders could now be made from plastic. Special courses to learn to play the instrument were held. Children in school were taught to play the recorder and it became, and still is, a great favourite. The recorder is often the first instrument to be played by pupils.

Arnold Dolmetsch always shared his enthusiasm for old instruments with his whole family, and together they joined in music-making on various instruments of earlier centuries.

After Arnold Dolmetsch's death in 1940, his son Carl took charge of the workshops which his father had set up. Recorders, harpsichords, lutes and other old instruments, still made at Haslemere, are bought by professional musicians and other enthusiasts in this and other countries.

Music in the Home

In the early part of the twentieth century, music was reaching a much wider public. Greater facilities were provided for the training of professional and amateur musicians. Many more opportunities were available to hear music live or on the radio. But music-making in the home, for family entertainment, was on the decrease.

7
Jazz, Pop
and All That

Perhaps a change in the character of popular music became most apparent in England in the 1920s. After the restrictions of the First World War, a new freedom emerged. A lively dance called the Charleston became almost a craze. Other new dances were the Tango, the Foxtrot and the Quickstep. The Viennese Waltz was slowed down, and became the Modern Waltz.

47   The Charleston was one of the dances which marked a breaking away from sedateness. This cartoon shows that the shorter ladies' dresses of the 1920s allowed the Charleston to be performed with liveliness.

▼

Ragtime and Jazz

But earlier, at the turn of the century, a new rage had swept America, and it eventually came to England. It was Ragtime. Ragtime originated as the music of the American Negro. As it developed, it was mostly played on the piano. The music was published, so that anyone could buy a copy of a favourite ragtime melody and learn to play it on the piano. Eventually, ragtime bands appeared, only to be replaced by jazz in the 1920s.

Both ragtime and jazz are syncopated; that is, the normal beat of the music is displaced. Another beat in the bar is accented instead. This transfers the normal rhythm of the piece to another point. But there was

The Girl of the straight legs. "IT'S A PITY YOU DON'T CHARLESTON, AUDREY. YOUR KNEES ARE SIMPLY MADE FOR IT."

48 The Savoy Hotel Orpheans Band, which was one of the foremost in London. The soloist is playing a saxophone, as is the musician in the bottom right-hand corner. Most of the players in the top bands were expert performers on more than one instrument. In this picture, some second instruments can be seen near the performers.

a big difference. Whereas the music of ragtime was written down, the music of jazz was not.

In jazz, it is the solo musician who improvises a melodic line over a theme, while a syncopated rhythm is played by the other instrumentalists. In the mid-1930s, a new item was introduced into a jazz programme, called a Jam Session. In this, all the players in the jazz band extemporise at the same time. Jazz music is brisk and lively, syncopated and rhythmic.

At first, the instruments used in a jazz band included the saxophone, violin, piano, banjo, drums and various improvised instruments like motor horns and whistles.

As jazz developed, one usual combination of instruments was a clarinet (which played the parts originally taken by the violin), saxophone, trombone, drums and piano. The

sombre tone of a muted trumpet was often included. The saxophone became very important in jazz bands. This instrument, which is seldom heard in symphony orchestras, has the single reed of the clarinet and the conical tube of the oboe.

Many jazz bands were formed in England, both professional and amateur. Not all played "true" jazz. The syncopated rhythm of jazz was often featured, but the improvisation was not always included. Each band developed its own individual style and the repertoire included soft, sweet music. The rhythm was always strict, and the music was therefore very suitable for dancing.

Slowly, the music of jazz began to change. One variation introduced in the 1920s was the Blues, which was a rhythmic song or dance, rather slow and melancholy.

Swing became popular in the 1930s. In this, improvisation is carried out in turn by different instruments in the band. It has different forms, but usually the rhythm of the tune is disturbed by the introduction of rubato. In rubato, the time of the music is distorted by slowing down at one point and immediately speeding up, so that the correct total time is taken. The Italian word "rubato"

▲

49   During the Second World War Christopher
Stone became a Major in the Army, but he was still
able to broadcast on the radio. Here he is seen
broadcasting to Forces in overseas hospitals and
convalescent homes.

means "robbed" or "stolen", but in the case
of music it must be paid back by the end of
the phrase.

Later in the 1930s, Boogie-Woogie and
Bebop (or Bop) became fashionable. Boogie-
Woogie has a definite pattern or harmony,
whereas Bebop is mainly based on modern
harmony with dissonant chords. In all forms
of jazz, it is the spontaneous playing of the

▲

50   Henry Hall. His voice was as well-known as
his face. At the end of a radio broadcast his final
spoken words and the band's closing tune were the
same — "Here's to the next time".

performer which is dominant, rather than
the composition itself.

The number of instrumentalists in the
professional jazz bands increased, and most
of the leading bands became attached to
large hotels, especially in London. Some
played at famous dance halls, like the
Hammersmith Palais de Danse.

The band leaders became very popular
figures. They included Jack Hylton, Billy
Cotton, Ray Noble, Jack Payne, Ambrose
and Henry Hall. The elegant decor of the

hotel or the dance hall set the scene and gave an impression of affluence. The musicians were smartly dressed and well-groomed.

Professional bands were copied by amateurs, who played for dances in local village halls and church rooms.

Throughout the 1930s, the recession hit most families in some way. Whenever it was possible, people were glad to indulge in escapism by listening and dancing to the bands and imagining how things might be.

As the new music became popular, so the number of instruments in a group became larger. The term "orchestra" began to be used, although the combination of instruments was very different to that of a symphony orchestra.

The dance bands and orchestras often included a singer. A special kind of singing called "crooning" reached England from the United States. By the mid-1940s, it was an established part of modern music. This sweet, soft, sentimental type of vocalism was featured several times during an evening's programme.

Jazz music and its variations were popularized by gramophone records and by broadcasts over the radio. During the 1930s and the Second World War Christopher Stone presented a record request programme. He was the forerunner of the disc jockey, although he was never referred to as such, and presented the records in a very different style. Many people asked him to play records of the new modern music.

During the experimental days of radio, the London Radio Dance Band broadcast live programmes. In 1928, the BBC replaced this small group with the larger BBC Dance Orchestra. For four years the orchestra's leader was Jack Payne. In 1932, he was succeeded by Henry Hall. The BBC Dance Orchestra was very successful, and its popularity lasted for about twenty years.

Pop Music

By the 1960s popular music, the music of the ordinary people, had changed dramatically, and affectionately became known as "Pop". The soft, sweet music gradually disappeared.

The larger bands were superseded by an enormous number of small groups. Different instruments were used. The saxophone was replaced by several kinds of guitar. Almost every group featured the electric guitar, the vibrant sound of which is produced by electricity. Drums and other percussion instruments maintained their popularity. It became usual for all members of the group to sing, either individually or together. But the soft, sentimental crooning had gone. The vocals still sang of love, but in a louder, harsher outpouring. The formal titles of the bands also vanished, to be replaced by witty, folky names like "The Rolling Stones" or "Cream".

Gone, too, were the well-groomed musicians in their well-pressed suits. They were replaced by shaggy youths in denim jeans and casual open-necked shirts, or the gaudy glitter of a sequin-spangled outfit. The pop singers became fashion-leaders.

With astonishing suddenness, in the 1960s, England became the focal centre of the world of pop. The Beatles came on the scene.

Four youths from Liverpool started singing and playing together in their home town in a club called "The Cavern". They sang and played their own pop music. John Lennon was the group's lead and rhythm guitarist, Paul McCartney played the bass guitar, George Harrison the lead guitar and Ringo Starr the drums. John Lennon and Paul McCartney wrote their songs, which eventually included titles like "Please, please me", "She loves you" and "Yellow Submarine". By 1962, the four young men had gained national popularity as a quartet. They soon had their own radio programme, *Pop go the Beatles* and also broadcast on *Saturday Club*.

Pop music became a craze. The adoration of the Beatles and their music amounted at times to mass hysteria. The première of their

51   The Beatles, at the height of their popularity, as they appeared on television. Note that Paul McCartney plays his instrument in an unconventional way, with the normal use of the left and right hand reversed.

first film "A Hard Day's Night", in 1964, caused a stampede in Piccadilly Circus, London, when more than ten thousand teenagers gathered outside the London Pavilion hoping to catch a glimpse of their four idols.

Pop was popular and had come to stay. It became the craze of young people to attend concerts and hear pop live, after which they would buy records of their favourite performers.

As the new music spread, discos began to take the place of more formal dances. At a disco, pop music records are played, although a group sometimes supplies the music. The sound is amplified and reproduced at a fairly high volume. In the semi-darkness, flashing lights of red, yellow, blue and green mesmerise the participants as they perform unscripted steps.

Many enthusiasts prefer to listen to a performance and to watch the often unwieldy gyrations of the performing group of pop musicians.

Some pop fans attend pop festivals which take place from time to time. Some of these are held out of doors and large numbers who are attracted are prepared to camp out in order to hear their favourite groups. Unfortunately, this kind of gathering is sometimes associated with drug-taking, which may give the pop festivals a disreputable name. The respectability of the concerts in the Vauxhall, Ranelagh and Marylebone Gardens of the eighteenth and nineteenth centuries and of the bandstand concerts on the seaside promenades has been replaced by noisy music appreciated by thousands of jeans-clad young people.

The new music brought a lively, free rhythmic beat and song, reminiscent of some of the old folk music. Different variations developed, like Rock and Roll, Rhythm and Blues, and Country and Western.

Country and Western originated in America many years ago as a form of folk music. Its songs often begin happily, but then introduce an element of pathos or tragedy. It spread to England, and from the 1960s onward, Country and Western music expanded rapidly. Various types include Old Time, Rockabilly and Gospel.

Although Country and Western is sometimes associated with groups, the music is often performed by a soloist singing while playing a guitar.

The new folk music differs greatly from the original English tunes collected by Cecil Sharp and his colleagues. Many amateurs became interested in the modern folk music with its element of pop. There was a resultant upsurge in the 1960s in the demand for guitar lessons.

Modern Musicals

A great change has taken place in musical productions in the theatre. They are no longer termed "Musical Comedies", but "Musicals". The title is an accurate description, since the successors of *The Bohemian Girl* and *Maritana* are often of a much more serious nature, although the music is modern and lively. The titles include *Oliver*, adapted from Charles Dickens' story of the boy raised in the workhouse. Even religious themes, like the Biblical story of *Joseph and his Amazing Technicolour Dreamcoat*, feature lively pop music rather than the sombre tones formerly associated with the Church.

Pop Music and the Church

The pop element has infiltrated into church music. Religious songs of the Third World, with their native beat, have been introduced. Songs like the traditional African "Kum ba yah" and the "Caribbean Lord's Prayer" are sung to a guitar, while the church congregation, usually consisting of young people, joins in.

The Church was quick to react to the introduction of pop music. Volumes of modern hymns including pop or folk

52 The Biblical story of *Joseph and his Amazing Technicolour Dreamcoat* is now a lively, modern musical.

tunes have been produced. These have titles like *Youth Praise*.

Like the old folk songs, modern music includes songs with a story or a message. Sometimes these are of a religious nature. It is not unusual for a guitar-playing group to sing an item during a normal church service. Even cathedrals and abbeys, the bastions of traditional church music, occasionally hold a Rock Mass. But, generally speaking, at present, pop music has become only a small part of the music in church worship.

Electronic Organs

In church music, economic considerations have forced many parishes to replace a pipe organ with an electronic model, rather than face the enormous cost of repairing the original instrument. Although the modern development of electronic church organs now makes them more acceptable, many congregations prefer the traditional pipe organ, and make the upkeep and repair of their pipe organ a priority.

It is in the secular sector that electronic organs have become popular. Because they are compact and do not have cumbersome pipe-work, these organs fit easily into the home.

But are musical instruments about to disappear? Will they be replaced by synthesizers? These computer-controlled machines imitate "human" music, but the synthesizer cannot convey personal feeling or emotion. In art and science the aim is always to reach perfection, but the synthesizer emits such a perfect rhythm that the result almost amounts to a dull monotony.

Music Round the World

During the last few decades, air travel has brought far-away nations into closer touch with each other and people of various nationalities now mingle. As a result, American and African influences have merged into the popular music of England as the rhythms, harmonies and instruments of these and other countries become known.

53   An electronic organ, which has no cumbersome pipe work, gives enjoyment to this performer, who plays the instrument in his own home.

▼

8
Classical Music Today

Learning to Play

While many young people play pop music today, a great number also enjoy classical music. Many learn to play various instruments. In schools, lessons are given to pupils from a very early age. Children learn to play one or more instruments — the recorder, guitar, percussion and many orchestral instruments including the violin, trumpet and clarinet.

Youth orchestras are active, not only in schools, but in counties. The most proficient of the instrumentalists are chosen to play in the National Youth Orchestra of Great Britain. This orchestra was the idea of Ruth Railton, who first formed it in 1947. Its members are young musicians between sixteen and nineteen years of age. Rehearsals and the culminating concerts take place three times a year in different towns. The orchestra of one hundred and fifty players is selected from about 2,000 applicants and meets during school holidays. The players are trained by expert instrumentalists and have the experience of playing under leading conductors.

Other children, and also adults, study privately. Some measure their progress by taking the examinations of various examining bodies. One of these, the Associated Board, is an amalgamation of the Royal Academy of Music, the Royal College of Music, the Royal Northern College of Music and the Royal Scottish Academy of Music. The original alliance between the Royal Academy of Music and the Royal College of Music took place in 1889. It was intended to provide a reliable progression of examinations which would give a sound foundation of musicianship. This was an endeavour to put an end to the activities of various dubious examination bodies which were active at that time.

As young people grow up, they often continue to practise their music-making. Membership of amateur operatic societies, choral societies, church choirs, amateur orchestras and music societies all give opportunities to enjoy music.

Professional Musicians

For those who choose to become professional musicians there are more opportunities for training and performance than were available in earlier centuries. Much more encouragement is given to the young musician.

On the other hand, competition between musicians is very great. The professional performer of today must carry a far larger repertoire than in earlier centuries. It is necessary to achieve a higher degree of per-

54   Part of the string section of the National Youth Orchestra of Great Britain during a rehearsal for a concert.

fection in technical and interpretative skills than ever before. There must also be a willingness to play in all parts of the world, and this involves an enormous amount of travelling.

Radio, television, gramophone records and tape recording techniques have made it possible for both musician and ordinary listener to hear and compare the performance and interpretation of many kinds of music. Air travel enables performers to travel quickly from country to country. This means that audiences can hear a far greater number of "live" musicians than ever before.

A little over a century ago it was possible for a solo virtuoso to travel in this country and abroad for years, playing either Programme A or Programme B, probably replacing one item occasionally. This is not so today. The modern soloist must keep a careful check on which works he or she performs where and when, which are recorded and which are broadcast. The programmes must constantly be varied.

Young Musicians

Young musicians who are outstanding are given special opportunities to study and perform. In addition to going to the established academies, colleges and schools of music, a student may take a degree in music at many universities.

More recently, several new training centres have been formed. The Menuhin School in Surrey was one of these, and was founded in 1963 by the virtuoso violinist Yehudi Menuhin. Here, only the most gifted children and young people receive instruction.

Similarly, highly gifted pupils study at Chetham's School of Music in Manchester. This school was formed in 1969 and is housed in the buildings of the old Blue Coat Charity School near Manchester Cathedral.

The Menuhin School and Chetham's School of Music accept students from many parts of the world. Both day and boarding students attend, and while musical ability

and promise are the main qualifications for entry, general educational subjects must also be studied. On leaving, many go to music colleges or to university for further study.

Young musicians are able to take part in competitions from time to time. Those under nineteen years of age from all over Great Britain are eligible to try to gain the title "BBC TV Young Musician of the Year". The standard of this competition is extremely high. Various preliminary sessions are held before the televising of the competitions to find the winners of the four sections (piano, strings, woodwind, brass) and then the final competition which decides the outright winner. Michael Hext, a trombonist, was the first to achieve this honour in 1978, and Nicholas Daniel, an oboeist, was successful in the next competition in 1980. The winner of the third competition in 1982 was a pianist, Anna Markland.

Another very demanding competition for pianists is held every three years. It is the Leeds International Piano Competition. Pianists from all over the world compete in this competition. Ian Hobson was the winner in 1981. Part of the prize was a tour arranged for the winner to give concerts as a soloist and also with orchestras. Ian Hobson is now assured of a career as a successful virtuoso pianist.

Musical Festivals

Many different kinds of musical festivals are held throughout the country. Some of these are competitive, and those taking part include children (some quite small), potential professional musicians and talented adults. Certificates, medals, cups, rose bowls and other awards are given for the best performances.

Another form of musical festival is not competitive. People attend to hear favourite orchestras and internationally acclaimed soloists. Noted teachers give master classes to talented students; unusual instruments and forms of music are played. Recitals on old instruments, like the harpsichord, or the older wind instruments can be heard. New compositions, sometimes with unfamiliar experimental harmonies, are played, and often a new work is specially commissioned and given its first performance. But the outstanding works of the classical composers are not neglected, and different anniversaries are celebrated by special concerts.

People coming from a distance often stay during the whole period of the festival — a week or longer — and make the feast of music a stimulating holiday experience. Some of the larger festivals are held in London, Cheltenham, Bath and Edinburgh, although many more are held elsewhere on a smaller scale.

The oldest English musical festival continues to be popular today. The Three Choirs Festival first took place over 250 years ago. This festival is held annually by the cathedrals of Gloucester, Hereford and Worcester. The three cathedrals take it in

55 Anna Markland, the pianist, when she gained the award of BBC TV Young Musician of the Year.
▼

56   The scene during the Three Choirs Festival,
when it was the turn of Worcester Cathedral to be
the host.

rotation to be the host. The choirs join together and sing the services and other religious music in the cathedral whose turn it is to hold the festival. Other cathedrals, abbeys and churches also hold their own musical festivals.

The Arts Council

During the last half century much has been done to foster and encourage music-making throughout the country. In 1946, the Arts Council of Great Britain was formed under the auspices of the government. Its work was further extended in 1967, when a new charter was granted. This enabled the council not only to foster the arts, but to make grants to organizations engaged in music and other arts. Money is also given to subsidize various musical concerts and productions of opera and ballet. Those eligible to receive help range from nationally acclaimed organizations, down to local music societies.

57   The lovely Sussex garden setting of the Glyndebourne Opera House.
▼

Opera Today

With regard to opera, private individuals have also helped to establish and ensure regular performances. John Christie, the owner of a lovely estate in Sussex, opened the Glyndebourne Festival Theatre there in 1934. Glyndebourne specializes in opera performances of a very high standard, and the operas of Mozart are frequently given. People in London, eager to go to the lovely Sussex countryside and attend the opera, arranged for a special train to take them there.

By 1954, Glyndebourne Opera had become so well-established that John Christie created the Glyndebourne Arts Trust. This ensures that performances at his country estate will be perpetuated.

Another opera organization was created at Snape Maltings, Aldeburgh, in Suffolk, and is closely connected with Benjamin Britten (1913-76). Britten was one of the foremost English composers of the twentieth century. Among many other compositions, he wrote

operas, including *Peter Grimes*, *The Rape of Lucretia*, *The Turn of the Screw*, *Billy Budd* and *Noye's Fludd*. Britten's operas are very different from those of the earlier composers. They do not merely entertain, but are deep studies of the human environment, and give cause for a lot of serious thought.

In 1947, together with Peter Pears and John Crozier, Britten formed the English Opera Group for the performance of chamber operas. The following year they also founded the Aldeburgh Festival, which is held annually in June.

Composers Today

Today's composers still fulfil the progress begun by Elgar, Vaughan Williams and others. Two of the most notable are Sir William Walton (1902-1983) and Sir Michael Tippett (1905-   ). Both have written operas, symphonies, various orchestral works and other compositions.

Orchestras and Concerts

London is still the main centre for orchestral and other musical activity. Orchestras which are based in the capital include the Royal Philharmonic Orchestra, the London Symphony Orchestra and the BBC Symphony Orchestra. Among comparable orchestras in the provinces are the Hallé Orchestra in Manchester and the City of Birmingham Symphony Orchestra. Most orchestras from London and the provinces tour the country from time to time to give concerts.

The "Proms" are still thriving, although the concerts are no longer given in the Queen's Hall. This was destroyed by bombs in 1941 during the Second World War. Since then, the Sir Henry Wood Promenade Concerts have been held in the Royal Albert Hall, London. The last night of the Proms is always a very special occasion. It is a tradition that the *Fantasia on British Sea Songs* is played, and the audience joins the orchestra by lustily singing Dr Thomas Arne's old song

▲
58   Benjamin Britten at work on one of his compositions.

59 *Noye's Fludd*. Children play an important
part in this opera by Benjamin Britten.

60 The Barbican Centre Concert Hall, which
opened in London in 1982, and where symphony
concerts are regularly held.

"Rule, Britannia", which was first performed in 1740.

In 1951, a Festival of Britain was held. A magnificent concert hall, the Festival Hall, was built on the South Bank of the Thames. The Royal Festival Hall is a large concert hall, which has a fine organ. The building also has a smaller recital room called the Queen Elizabeth Hall.

Church Music

Gradual changes are taking place in music in the Church. The traditional church music is incorporating the new freedoms of time signatures and unfamiliar harmonies. Perhaps congregations first notice this when listening to a modern composer's powerful, sometimes discordant, organ voluntary. In the Anglican church, the introduction of the new Alternative Service Book will doubtless bring new musical settings of the modern services. The music of Dr Herbert Howells (1892-1983) is frequently used in cathedral services, although his compositions are not limited to church music only.

One remarkable addition to the old historical church tradition has taken place in recent years. In 1973, a Choir School was formed at Tewkesbury Abbey in Gloucestershire. Based on the same principles as the ancient cathedral and university choir schools founded centuries ago, Tewkesbury Abbey Choir School is one of the few cathedral choir schools founded since the Reformation, and is the most recent.

There have been periods when church music has been sadly neglected, but now, although financial, staffing and other difficulties still remain, the quality of playing and singing in English cathedrals is very high.

Change and Innovation

The world of music is, like everything else, subject to change. The D'Oyly Carte Opera Company, with its traditional presentation of the Gilbert and Sullivan operas, ceased to exist in 1982. In the same year, a magnificent new Arts complex, the Barbican Centre, opened in London. It has a superb concert hall for the performance of music, and modern technology has attempted to make the acoustics as perfect as possible.

While all this practical music-making is taking place, present-day composers are exploring new forms and techniques. Popular music is not the only field in which experimentation takes place. In classical music new devices are being tried. Certainly some experimentation is included, and only part of the result can be termed real progress or even true music.

Music is now composed which includes intervals smaller than the semitone. Until recently the semitone was the smallest interval in general use. These new intervals are called microtones and are often quarter-tones or even smaller. Instead of having the usual twelve semitones, the octave can now contain a far greater number of smaller intervals. To the untuned ear, this kind of

61 Modern music often does not keep the same time signature for long. This short example from Webern's *Variations for Orchestra* (Op. 30, bars 15-20) changes four times.

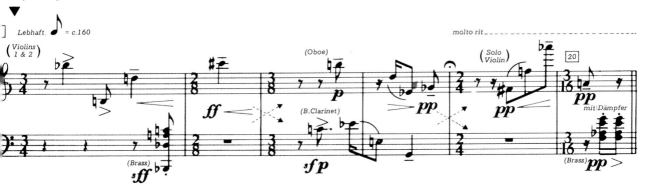

music can sound strange. Only after repeated listening and study does the music become acceptable. Even then, many works written in this style are discarded.

Another innovation is to write music which is not in any particular key. Music where the key is absent is termed "atonal".

Traditional practice is also changing with regard to time signatures. Normally the same time (for example, three beats in a bar) is kept during a whole piece of music. Now it is becoming quite common to find that, in new music, the time signature changes at any point. This disturbs the steady rhythm of the piece.

In any age, all new music is an experiment. Some efforts are immediately discarded. Some achieve immediate popularity, but are short-lived. Other compositions may be ahead of their time and not acceptable to people of that period. If the same music is tested again later — sometimes centuries later — it may then be acclaimed because people understand it more and their ears are more readily attuned to it. Only time will tell which music is transient and which will pass the test of time by having lasting qualities.

This book traces a path through the history and development of music and musicians. But music has many interesting paths, with numerous diversions. Many more journeys in music must be made by reading, listening and performing.

Some Key Dates

1135 (or earlier)   The Chapel Royal founded

1591   *My Lady Nevell's Booke* compiled

1650   *Playford's English Dancing Master* published

1709   Cristofori invents the piano

1728   *The Beggar's Opera* produced in London

1732   Covent Garden Theatre, London, built

1742   Handel's *Messiah* first performed

1813   The Philharmonic Society, London, founded

1829   Robert Wornum, Jnr. invents the upright piano

1867-1896   The Gilbert and Sullivan operas written

1870   Education Act: ensures that all children, including choristers, receive a good general education

1878   The Salvation Army founded by William Booth

1895   Henry J. Wood appointed to conduct the Promenade Concerts

1898   The Folk Song Society formed

1920s   Synchronised sound films produced

1922   British Broadcasting Company formed

1924   Henry Walford Davies broadcasts the first music lesson to schools

1946   The Arts Council of Great Britain formed

1947   The National Youth Orchestra of Great Britain formed

1951   The Festival Hall opened in London

1960s   "Pop" and the Beatles become the rage

1982   The Barbican Centre in London opened

Glossary

acoustics the qualities of the transmission of sound in a building.

ballad a song, the words of which often tell a historical, fantastic or sentimental story.

baton the stick with which a conductor may direct the orchestra.

canon the word means "rule". The rule is that several voices must sing together but must follow each other after the same short space of time, each singing the same melody.

concerto a composition in which one or more solo instruments play with an orchestra.

concordant (or *consonant*) a sound which is harmonious and satisfying to listen to. The opposite of discordant.

discordant (or *dissonant*) a sound which is jarring to listen to. The opposite of concordant.

ensemble a group of instrumentalists or singers performing together, each usually having an individual part.

florid applied to a rapid progression of notes, often brilliant and ornamented.

harmony notes sounding together in an acceptable pattern.

hoboies (or *hautboy*) an old form of the oboe.

impresario the manager of a theatre or opera company.

intone to sing on one note.

libretto the words of an opera, oratorio or other musical work.

masque a spectacular musical and artistic presentation staged by the aristocracy. Popular during the seventeenth century. Originally, the performers were disguised by wearing masks.

microtone very small interval of music of less than a semitone.

octave a scale of eight notes, the eighth note sounding the same as the first at a higher level.

ornaments musical decorations; turns, trills, grace notes and other embellishments inserted into a melody.

parody to copy the style of a work, inserting words which will mimic and ridicule.

patron one who supports and encourages, usually giving financial assistance.

recitative a short passage or sentence, usually preceding an operatic aria. The words are sung in the rhythm of speech, and the tune tends to follow the inflexion of the words.

repertoire the list of compositions which can be included in a programme.

sackbut an early instrument; the forerunner of the trombone.

sacred connected with religion and the

church. The opposite of secular.

scales   the ordered progression of notes.

score   music set out to show all the parts of the composition on the same page, as they will be performed together.

secular   applicable to ordinary life, in contrast to having a religious connection. The opposite of sacred.

semitone   an interval of half a tone. There are twelve semitones in an octave.

shawm   a forerunner of the oboe.

synchronize   to fit in at the same time.

syncopate   to disturb the normal beat in a composition.

tempo   the speed at which a piece of music is played.

theme   a melody which is repeated regularly in a composition.

unison   several voices singing or instruments playing the same notes.

virtuoso   one who is exceptionally skilled, especially in playing a musical instrument.

Books for Further Reading

Anna Alston and Julia Boyd-Dobson,
Working in the World of Music,
Batsford 1982

René Clemencic,
Old Musical Instruments,
Weidenfeld & Nicolson, 1968

Ernest Closson,
History of the Piano,
Paul Elek, 1974

David Cox,
The Henry Wood Proms,
British Broadcasting Corporation, 1980

Helen Erickson,
A Young Person's Guide to the Opera,
Macdonald, 1980

Imogen Holst,
Holst,
Faber and Faber, 1974

Alan Kendall,
Benjamin Britten,
Macmillan, 1973

Stanley Sadie,
Handel,
Faber and Faber, 1968

Keith Spence,
Living Music,
Hamish Hamilton, 1979

Index

The numbers in **bold type** refer to the figure numbers of the illustrations